Writing as Meditation

Journal & Guidebook

BUILDING YOUR BOOK WITH ATTENTION AND INTENTION

Writing as Meditation

Journal & Guidebook

BUILDING YOUR BOOK WITH ATTENTION
AND INTENTION

Caroline Smith

Tandem Light Press
950 Herrington Rd.
Suite C128
Lawrenceville, GA 30044

Copyright © 2019 by Caroline Smith

All rights reserved. No part of this book may be reproduced, scanned, or transmitted in any printed, electronic, mechanical, including photocopying, recording, or any information storage and retrieval system, without permission in writing from the publisher. Please do not participate in or encourage piracy of copyrighted materials in violation of the author's rights.

Tandem Light Press paperback edition November 2019

ISBN: 978-1-7341261-4-3
Library of Congress Control Number: 2019952324

PRINTED IN THE UNITED STATES OF AMERICA

This Journal Belongs To:

Contents

Introduction	ix
Part I: Building Your Book	**1**
Foundational Necessities	3
Target Audience	5
Value Proposition & Purpose	7
Synopsis	9
Fiction	11
Non-Fiction	17
Marketing	21
Part II: Journal	**23**
About the Author	**281**

Introduction

Over the years, I've been shown how valuable meditation can be; not only in our every day lives, but also in the creation of books. You see, meditation, like writing, is a craft—a practice. We won't start out being great at either one. Your first draft will never be the next great American Novel, and the first time you sit down to meditate, you won't immediately float into nirvana just by saying "Om" and sitting on a cushion. Both of these practices take work. And we will get out of each one exactly what we put in.

What Mediation is Not

Meditation is not a cure-all for all of the things going wrong in your life. Nor is it an immediate problem-solver. We can include things like the power of positive thinking in our daily meditations, but that's not the overall focus of meditation. So what is it? Well…that depends. (Which, as you may or may not know, is my answer to almost everything in writing and publishing).

Specifically, that depends on what you hope to get out of meditation. Do you want to quiet the ever-chittering "monkey mind" of worry and anxiety? Do you want to be more introspective? Do you want to tap into your higher, creative self? Do you simply want to attain some modicum of peace and quiet in your every day life? All of these things can be achieved with meditation. And the best part is, it's always there and can help us achieve all of these and more. That's also why we call it a practice. It will evolve as we evolve and serve different purposes at different points in our lives.

What Meditation Is

Simply put, meditation is focusing only on one thing for a certain period of time. I bet you're thinking to yourself that you do this all the time, you just never thought of it as meditation. We talk about athletes getting into "the zone," which, is essentially, a form of meditation. Any time you have been doing something where your mind and body are focused only on the task in front of you, whether it's a toddler, painting, running, cooking, work, or writing, that's meditation.

The act of being meditative isn't hard. It isn't challenging, or it isn't meant to be. I've taught meditation workshops where people come in and say they've tired meditation before but they didn't stick with it, because they couldn't get their brain to stop thinking about things. Which is exactly the reason they should continue mediating, not stop. No one expects for you to clear your mind and think of nothing the first time you do this. So let's let go of that expectation first.

Meditation should be as easy as breathing. In fact, most meditations that you might find in podcasts, online, or in workshops will have you start out by doing breathing exercises. Mostly that's because deep breaths help center and ground our mind and body for the work we are about to do; the focus and attention we're about to give. The breath helps us make space for the deep work that's about to happen and helps us calm our body so that we can prepare to create, or be introspective, or simply make space for being quiet.

Using this Book in Your Practice

I recommend to all of my authors that they keep a writing journal and that's partly what this guidebook is intended to be. It will help you to stay on the path for your book and really zero in on what it is you're trying to create, whether that's fiction or non-fiction.

I also ask all of my authors to set aside fifteen minutes a day in pursuit of their book. Meaning, you don't have to be actually writing for that time but do something to help your book along: create a character sheet, meditate on marketing, or pray for financial prosperity. These fifteen minutes are the most important investment you can make in your book, so do yourself a favor and turn off your phone, put a Do Not Disturb sign on your office door, and focus only on what you want to accomplish in those fifteen minutes (or more if you can find them).

This book was designed with those fifteen minutes in mind. You get to decide how much or how little attention you devote to it every day. There is a front section designed to help you focus on your book's content and then the back is just lined pages for you to jot ideas down.

If you find that you need more direction, I invite you to listen to my podcast: Inspiration to Publication, or take my online course, also called

Inspiration to Publication, dedicated to new authors and their writing and publishing journey. Links for both can be found on my website.

Thank you for your time, attention, and dedication to your project. Please don't ever hesitate to reach out if you have questions or need assistance.

Happy writing!

Part I:

Building Your Book

Foundational Necessities

First things first. *Inhale. Exhale.* Take five deep breaths. Make sure the phone is on silent and you're somewhere you won't be disturbed.

When you're first starting your book, it's hard to know where to begin. On one side of the coin, I usually tell people to *just start writing*. But that's after three considerations have been made: 1) Target Audience, 2) Value Proposition, 3) Purpose. The following pages will help explain and explore these core, foundational ideas.

Target Audience: This is the group of people for whom you are writing, and you need to keep them in mind before you even begin writing. Often, we are our own target audience meaning we are writing a book for people like us. When I ask authors who their target audience is, I often hear the reply, "everyone." I involuntarily cringe every time that's the response. We can't be all things to all people, and we can't make everyone happy; we aren't pizza. So you find the bullseye. What do I mean by that? Imagine a target. In the very center—the bullseye—is your target audience. If you're writing a romance novel, your target audience is probably women between the ages of twenty-five to fifty-five. That's certainly not to say you can't reach men in the same age range, but they lie on the outer rings of the target. Make sense? This target audience will also determine your marketing strategy, which is why it's so important to determine early in the process.

Value Proposition: What is your reader gaining from the book? Knowledge, education, an escape? Think about what you want them to take away from it when they finish. This is the mentality of "what's in it for me?" as far as your readers are concerned.

Purpose: Why are you writing this book? Is it to publish just so you can say you're published? To give copies only to families and friends? To make money? To leave a legacy? Often, your value proposition helps you discover your purpose, also known as your "why."

Let's spend some time meditating on these three foundations.

Target Audience

My target audience is: _____ (Male or Female)?

They're _____ - _____ years old.

They live in _____ (cities, suburbs, small towns, etc.)

They work at _____ (Forbes, At Home, etc.)

Their favorite type of food is _____ and they eat it _____ a _____ (once a week? once a day?

Their greatest fear is _____.

heir greatest achievement is _____.

As a hobby, or to relax or blow off steam they _____.

Other types of books or authors they enjoy are: _____

They dream about accomplishing _____ before they retire or turn 70.

I want them to feel _____ when they read my book.

Fill in any other aspects you'd like to consider about your target audience below.

_____

_____

_____

_____

Value Proposition & Purpose

Based on the previous pages, provide a summary of your target audience. Keep in mind that you need to try to be as specific as possible. You can always reach the rings outside the center of your bullseye, but we really want to aim for that as much as we can.

What is your value proposition? What is your book offering to your readers?

What is your purpose? Your purpose can also be identified as your "why."

Who is going to write your book? If you choose an author coach or ghostwriter, be sure to interview and find the *right one* for you, your personality, your timeline, and your project.

Synopsis

Jot down a general idea or synopsis of your book. For fiction and memoirs, include a general idea of setting, characters, plot, and what the conflict is. For non-fiction, think about why you're qualified to write this book and list major topics you want to include. Highlight or underline important keywords.

Fiction

If you're writing non-fiction, with the exception of a memoir, you can skip this page. Or, meditate on how you might include some of these ideas in your book.

There are three main components to any good fiction book, according to Diana Gabaldon, creator of the *Outlander* series: character, conflict, and consistency. After all of the fiction, non-fiction, children's books, and especially romance novels I've read and edited in the last several decades, I think she's completely correct. Whatever world you're building in your fiction, we want our characters to at least be sympathetic, and even if they aren't human, possess qualities that we can relate to as humans.

If you're writing a memoir, I want you to consider telling your life story as a novel. It will help keep the right theme, pacing, and storytelling elements to make it a good page-tuner if you keep that in mind.

Characters

Take some deep breaths here. This is the most fun part of novel-creation, but also where we tend to get the most lost as writers.

Close your eyes after you read this and visualize your main character. What do they look like? What is their best quality? What is their worst? What physical characteristics do they have? What are their hobbies? What is their internal need? What is their external goal? What is their misbelief that other characters will help correct? What is their motivation? What is their most closely guarded secret?

These questions are meant to get you in the right mindset of character-building. Feel free to come up with your own. Spend at least fifteen minutes creating this character on the lines below.

Secondary Character

Ask yourself the same questions above for your antagonist or secondary character. Are they good? Evil? How do they relate to the main character? How do they contrast the main character? Use some of the same questions for your main character and devise a characterization sheet for your secondary character.

Sub-characters

Who else needs to be included in the story? The snarky best friend? The main character's sister? The bad guy. Spend some time on these next few pages writing down ideas (that can always change) for up to eight sub-characters. If you find you don't have enough room here, you can always move into Part II.

Conflict

This can be a little bit tricky, but conflict is what propels the story forward. Conflict is where drama happens. Every chapter should include some element of the conflict. In other words: what is the problem? What is the main character trying to accomplish, achieve, or fix in every scene? Why can't they achieve it? What personal, inner issues are going to be tested by the plot and the main conflict?

Some of these questions won't be necessary until you actually begin writing, but because the conflict is part of the reason the book exists, you should spend at least fifteen minutes today writing about it. Bullet points and incomplete sentences are always fine for this journal. Even if you don't have a complete thought about it, and least have an idea of a direction you'd like to go.

Consistency

Whatever world you're creating, you need to be consistent in it. I have edited books where the setting or main character's name changes halfway through the book. This section is intended to help keep you on track. Jot down ideas here for names, settings, anything in your world that you want to be sure you're being consistent with (i.e. character's car make and model, the type of home or business they're in, etc.)

You also need to ensure you're consistent with character traits. If your character is sassy and argumentative, it would be out of character for them to not argue when someone contradicts them or their passion. Feel free to jot character traits down here or in the appropriate character section.

Non-Fiction

Inhale. Exhale.
Breathe through the noise and chaos of your day.
Let it go. Time to write.

If you've met me, taken my course, or listened to my podcast, you know I'm not a fan of outlines. I've mentioned many times that only about thirty percent of people think in a linear fashion where outlines are actually useful. The rest of us have ideas that jump around from topic to topic, especially when we're writing.

That being said, for my non-fiction authors, I want you to utilize whatever you find most helpful. You can write a rough outline on the following pages, just jot down topics, bullet point a few words, or in a few pages you'll see a spot where you can do some mind mapping. Just keep in mind, there is no *one way* to write non-fiction.

You've told me on previous pages why you're a subject matter expert (SME) and why you want to write this book. I'd like you to spend at least fifteen minutes today writing down topics that you want to include in your book. Make sure they are relevant to your subject and that you *should* be writing on them as a SME.

Structure and Vocabulary

I'd also like you to think about the nature of your book. Is it a how to? Will you have actionable steps at the end of each chapter? Will you be writing to people who already are familiar with this topic (target audience)? Or will you be writing to people who are unfamiliar? This will determine the conversation you have with your audience in the book. Will you need to include a glossary for those who are new to the subject matter?

Spend the next few pages meditating on these questions.

Marketing

Surprised by this entry? I did mention that target audience would speak directly to marketing. And, no matter how you publish (self, traditional, vanity, ebook only, independent, post-modern, etc.), they will all want you to have some idea of marketing ideas you can be using. They will also, inevitably, ask if you have an email list. So. It is never too early to market your book or start talking about it. As soon as you decide you're going to write a book, tell the world. Not only will it help keep you accountable, it will also help create interest and interest means sales (if you want those).

Spend your fifteen minutes thinking about what you may need from a marketing perspective. You can always come back to these pages and add on as well. Do you need/have social media platforms? If yes, do you have one dedicated to your business and/or writing (an author page)? Do you have a way to capture emails (i.e. Mailchimp)? Do you have or need a website?

I should also mention that most of these items are free, but it wouldn't be a bad idea to create a budget either in these pages or on a spreadsheet. Once published, your book will become a business. I know, I know—cart, horse—but I do want you to create space for at least thinking about a budget. Despite what anyone says, no form of publishing is free.

Part II:

Journal

"If a story is in you it has to come out."

-William Faulkner

"It is the possibility of having a dream come true that makes life interesting."

-Paulo Cohelo, The Alchemist

"Start writing
no matter what.
The water doesn't flow
until the faucet is
turned on."

-Louis L'Amor

"You can always edit a bad page. You can't edit a blank page."

-Jodi Picoult

"Resist the temptation to edit. Finish the first draft, first."

-Caroline Smith

"Keep moving forward."

-Walt Disney

"Books are like Swiss Army Knives. They offer endless creative and revealing possibilities for those who like to interact with them."

-John Maxwell Hamilton

"You fail only if you stop writing."

-Ray Bradbury

About the Author

As an award-winning editor and author coach, Caroline Smith has had the honor of bringing over 300 books to life and publication. Her favorite genre to read, write, and edit is romance, with fantasy, true crime, and biographies in a three-way tie for second place. In 2014 she won an IPBA Gold Ben Franklin award in collaboration with one of her authors for editorial and design. To better assist her authors all over the world, she developed a podcast and online course, both called "Inspiration to Publication."

When she's not writing or editing, she can be found teaching workshops and classes on a range of topics from writing and publishing to meditation and natural wellness while also getting her master's in Creative Writing from Queens University. Caroline is the author of Perspective Parenting: A Guide for the Modern Single Mom. She currently resides in the mountains of North Georgia with her three wild children, three goats, six bunnies, two dogs, and a cat.

To contact Caroline, please visit her website:
editorcaroline.com

www.ingramcontent.com/pod-product-compliance
Lightning Source LLC
Chambersburg PA
CBHW081227080526
44587CB00022B/3850